The Secret Of God's Love

The Secret Of God's Love

ANDREW MURRAY

Whitaker House

THE SECRET OF GOD'S LOVE

ISBN: 0-88368-549-3
Printed in the United States of America
Copyright © 1982 by Whitaker House

Whitaker House
30 Hunt Valley Circle
New Kensington, PA 15068

1 2 3 4 5 6 7 8 9 10 11 12 / 06 05 04 03 02 01 00 99 98

PREFACE

I have felt the need to write something that young
Christians might easily understand, and something
which might help them to be successful in their
Christian life. It is at this time especially that they
often encounter the principle temptations and fail-
ures of the Christian life. The nearness, all-
sufficiency, and faithfulness of the Lord Jesus, along
with the naturalness and fruitfulness of a life of faith
are so revealed that it seems one could say with
confidence, "Let the parable enter into my heart,
and all will be right."

May the blessed Lord give the blessing. May He
teach us to study the mystery of the Vine in the spirit
of worship, waiting for God's own teaching.

CONTENTS

Chapter One

THE VINE

"I am the true vine"—John 15:1.

All earthly things are shadows of heavenly realities. They are the expression, in created, visible forms, of God's invisible glory. The Life and the Truth are in heaven. On earth, we have figures and shadows of these heavenly truths. When Jesus says, "I am the *true* Vine," He tells us that all the vines of earth are pictures and emblems of Himself. He is the divine reality, of which they are the created expression. They all point to Him, preach Him, and reveal Him. If you want to know Jesus, study the vine.

Many eyes have gazed on and admired a great vine with its beautiful fruit. Come and gaze on the heavenly Vine until your eye turns from all else to admire Him. Many who live in a sunny climate sit and rest under the shadow of a vine. Come and be still under the shadow of the true Vine, and rest under it from the heat of the day. What countless numbers rejoice in the fruit of the vine! Come, take, and eat of the heavenly fruit of the true Vine. Let your soul say, "I sat under His shadow with great delight, and His fruit was sweet to my taste."

I am the true Vine. This is a heavenly mystery. The earthly vine can teach you much about this Vine of heaven. Many interesting and beautiful points of comparison suggest themselves. They help us to understand what Christ meant. But, such thoughts do not teach us to know what the heavenly Vine really is, in its cooling shade, and its life-giving fruit. The experience of this is part of the hidden mystery, which no one but Jesus Himself—by the Holy Spirit—can unfold and impart.

I am the true Vine. The vine is the living Lord, who Himself speaks and gives and works all that He has for us. If you want to know the meaning and power of that word, do not look for it in thought or study. These may help to show what you need from Him in order to awaken desire, hope, and prayer. But, they cannot show you the Vine. Jesus alone can reveal Himself. He gives His Holy Spirit to open the eyes to gaze upon Himself, to open the heart to receive Himself. He must Himself speak the word to you and me.

I am the true Vine. And what am I to do if I want the mystery, in all its heavenly beauty and blessing, opened up to me? With what you already know of the parable, bow down and be still. Worship and wait until the divine word enters your heart, and you feel His holy presence with you—in you. The over-shadowing of His holy love will give you the perfect calm and rest of knowing that the Vine will do all.

I am the true Vine. He who speaks is God—in His infinite power able to enter into us. He is man—one with us. He is the crucified One, who won a perfect righteousness and a divine life for us through His death. He is the glorified One, who, from the throne, gives His Spirit to make His presence real and true. He speaks. Oh, listen, not only to His words, but to Himself as He whispers secretly day by day, "I am the true Vine! All that the Vine can ever be to its branch, *I will be to you.*"

Holy Lord Jesus, the heavenly Vine of God's own planting, I beseech You, reveal Yourself to my soul. Let the Holy Spirit, not only in thought, but in experience, teach me all that You, the Son of God, are to me as the true Vine.

Chapter Two

THE HUSBANDMAN

"And my Father is the husbandman"—John 15:1.

A vine must have a husbandman to plant and watch over it, to receive and rejoice in its fruit. Jesus says, "My Father is the husbandman." He was the Vine of God's planting. All He was and did, He owed to the Father. In all, He only sought the Father's will and glory. He had become man to show us what relationship we ought to have with our Creator. He took our place, and the spirit of His life before the Father is what He continually seeks to make ours, "Of him, and through him, and to him, are all things" (Romans 11:36). He became the true Vine, that we might be true branches. In regard to both Christ and ourselves, the words teach us the two lessons of absolute dependence and perfect confidence.

My Father is the Husbandman. Christ always lived in the spirit of what He once said, "The Son can do nothing of himself" (John 5:19). As dependent as a vine is on a husbandman for its planting, fertilization, and care, Christ was entirely dependent on the Father for the wisdom and the strength to do the Father's will every day.

As He said in the previous chapter (John 14:10), "The words that I speak unto you I speak not of Myself: but the Father that dwelleth in me, he doeth the works." This absolute dependence had as its blessed counterpart the most blessed confidence that He had nothing to fear. The Father could not disappoint Him. With such a husbandman as His Father, He could enter death and the grave. He could trust God to raise Him up. All that Christ is and has, He has, not in Himself, but from the Father.

My Father is the Husbandman. That is as blessedly true of us as for Christ. Christ is about to teach His disciples about their being branches. Before He ever used the word, or speaks at all of abiding in Him or bearing fruit, He turns their eyes heavenward to the Father watching over them— working all in them. At the very root of all Christian life lies the thought that God is to do all. Our one work is to give and leave ourselves in His hands, in the confession of utter helplessness and dependence, in the assured confidence that He gives all we need. The great downfall of the Christian life is that, even where we trust Christ, we leave the Father out. Christ came to bring us to God, the Father. Christ lived the life of a man exactly as we have to live it. Christ the Vine points to God the Husbandman. As He trusted the Father, let us trust the Father. In that way, everything we ought to be and have, as those who belong to the Vine, will be given to us from above.

Isaiah said, "A vineyard of red wine; I the Lord do keep it; I will water it every moment: lest any hurt it, I will keep it night and day" (Isaiah 27:2-3). Before we begin to think of fruit or branches, let us have our heart filled with the faith: the Husbandman is as glorious as the Vine. As high and holy as is our calling, so mighty and loving is the God who will work it all. As surely as the Husbandman made the Vine what it was to be, will He make each branch what it is to be. Our Father is our Husbandman, the surety for our growth and fruit.

Blessed Father, we are Your husbandry. Oh, that You might have honor of the work of Your hands! O my Father, I desire to open my heart to the joy of this wondrous truth: My Father is the Husbandman. Teach me to know and trust You, and to see that the same deep interest with which You cared for and delighted in the Vine, extends to every branch—to me, too.

Chapter Three

THE BRANCH

"Every branch in me that beareth not fruit he taketh away"—John 15:2.

Here we have one of the chief words of the parable—*branch*. A vine needs branches. Without branches, it can do nothing; it can bear no fruit. It is equally as important to realize what the branch is as to know about the Vine and the Husbandman. Before we listen to what Christ has to say about it, let us first of all take in what a branch is. Let us consider what it teaches us of our life in Christ. A branch is simply a bit of wood, brought forth by the vine for the one purpose of serving it in bearing its fruit. It is of the very same nature as the vine, and has one life and one spirit with it. Just think for a moment about the lessons this suggests.

There is the lesson of *entire consecration*. The branch has only one reason for which it exists, one purpose to which it is entirely given up. That is, to bear the fruit the vine wishes to bring forth. And so, the believer has only one reason for his being a

15

branch—*one reason for his existence on earth*—that the heavenly Vine may bring forth His fruit through him. Happy is the soul that knows this, that has consented to it, and that says, "I have been redeemed and I live for one thing—as exclusively as the natural branch exists only to bring forth fruit, I too; as exclusively as the heavenly Vine exists to bring forth fruit, I too. As I have been planted by God into Christ, I have wholly given myself to bear the fruit that the Vine desires to bring forth."

There is the lesson of *perfect conformity*. The branch is exactly like the vine in every aspect—the same nature, the same life, the same place, the same work. In all this they are inseparably one. And so the believer needs to know that he is partaker of the divine nature. He must realize that he has the very nature and spirit of Christ in him, and that his one calling is to yield himself to a perfect conformity to Christ. The branch is a perfect likeness of the vine. The only difference is that the one is great and strong, and the source of strength, and that the other is little and feeble, ever needing and receiving strength. Likewise, the believer is—and is to be—the perfect likeness of Christ.

There is the lesson of *absolute dependence*. The vine has its stores of life and sap and strength, not for itself, but for the branches. The branches are, and have nothing but, what the vine provides and imparts. The believer is called to, and it is his highest blessedness to enter into, a life of entire and unceasing dependence upon Christ. Day and night, every

16

moment, Christ is to work in him all he needs.

And then there is the lesson of *undoubting confidence*. The branch has no care; the vine provides all; it has but to yield itself and receive. It is the knowledge of this truth that leads to the blessed rest of faith, the true secret of growth and strength, "I can do all things through Christ which strengtheneth me" (Philippians 4:13).

What a life we could have if we would just consent to be as branches! Dear child of God, learn the lesson. You have but one thing to do: only to be a branch—nothing more, nothing less! Just be a branch. Christ will be the Vine that gives all. And the Husbandman—the mighty God—who made the Vine what it is, *will as surely make the branch what it ought to be.*

Lord Jesus, reveal to me the heavenly mystery of the branch—in its living union with the Vine, in its claim on all its fullness. And, let Your all-sufficiency, holding and filling Your branches, lead me to rest in faith, knowing that You work all.

Chapter Four

THE FRUIT

"Every branch in me that beareth not fruit he taketh away"—John 15:2.

The next great word we have is fruit. The Vine, the Husbandman, the branch, the fruit. What does our Lord have to say to us of fruit? Simply this—that fruit is the one thing the branch is for. And, if it does not bear fruit, the husbandman takes it away. The vine is the glory of the husbandman. The branch is the glory of the vine. The fruit is the glory of the branch. If the branch does not bring forth fruit, there is no glory or worth in it. It is an offense and a hindrance, and the husbandman takes it away. The one reason for the existence of a branch—the one mark of being a true branch of the heavenly Vine, the one condition of being allowed by the divine Husbandman to share the life of the Vine—is the bearing of fruit.

And what is fruit? Something that the branch bears, not for itself, but for its owner. It is something that is to be gathered, and taken away. The branch does indeed receive sap from the vine for its own life, by which it grows thicker and stronger. But, this supply for its own maintenance is entirely subordinate to its fulfillment of the purpose of its existence—bearing fruit. It is because Christians do not understand or accept this truth that they so often fail in their efforts and prayers to live the branch life. They often desire it very earnestly. They read and meditate and pray, and yet they fail, and wonder why.

The reason is very simple: they do not know that *fruit bearing* is the *one thing they have been saved for*. Just as entirely as Christ became the true Vine in order to bear the fruit of life, you have been made a branch so as to bear fruit for the salvation of men.

The Vine and the branch are equally under the unchangeable law of fruit bearing as the one reason for their being. Christ and the believer, the heavenly Vine and the branch, both have their place in the world for one exclusive purpose—to carry God's saving love to men. Hence, the solemn word, "Every branch in me that beareth not fruit he taketh away."

Let us especially beware of one great mistake. Many Christians think their own salvation is the first thing. They think their earthly life and prosperity—with the care of their family—is second. And, what time and interest is left may then be devoted to fruitbearing—to the saving of men. No wonder that, in most cases, very little time or interest can be found. No, Christian, the one object with which you have been made a member of Christ's body is that the Head may have you to carry out His saving work. The one object God had in making you a branch is that Christ may bring life to men through you. Your personal salvation, your business and care for your family, *are entirely subordinate to this.* Your first aim in life—your first aim every day—should be to know how Christ desires to carry out His purpose in you.

Let us begin to think as God thinks. Let us accept Christ's teaching and respond to it. The one object of my being a branch—the one mark of my being a true branch, the one condition of my abiding and growing strong—is that I bear the fruit of the heavenly Vine for dying men to eat and live. And the one thing which I can be most perfectly assured of is that, with Christ as my Vine, and the Father as my Husbandman, I can indeed be a fruitful branch.

Our Father, You come seeking fruit. Teach us to realize how truly this is the one object of our existence, and of our union to Christ. Make it the one desire of our hearts to be branches, so filled with the Spirit of the Vine, as to bring forth fruit abundantly.

Chapter Five

MORE FRUIT

"And every branch that beareth fruit, he purgeth it, that it may bring forth more fruit"—John 15:2.

The thought of fruit is very prominent in the eyes of Him who sees things as they are. Fruit is so truly the one thing God has set His heart upon that our Lord, after having said that the branch which bears no fruit is taken away, adds: and where there is fruit, the one desire of the Husbandman is more fruit. As the gift of His grace, as the token of spiritual vigor, as the demonstration of the glory of God and Christ, and as the only way for satisfying the need of the world, God longs for more fruit.

More fruit. This is a very searching word. As churches and individuals, we are in danger of desiring self-contentment more than we are of anything else. The secret spirit of Laodicea—we are rich and abundant in goods, and have need of nothing—may exist even though we are not aware of it. The divine warning—poor and wretched and miserable—finds little recognition where it is most needed.

Let us not be content with the thought that we are taking an equal share with others in the work that is being done. Let us not rest in the thought that men are satisfied with our efforts in Christ's service, or even point to us as examples. Let our only desire be to know whether we are bearing all the fruit Christ is willing to give through us as living branches. Let us desire to rest in close and living union with Him, and to satisfy the loving heart of the great Husbandman, our Father in heaven, in His desire for more fruit.

More fruit. The word comes with divine authority to search and test our life. The true disciple will heartily surrender himself to its holy light. He will earnestly ask that God Himself show him what is lacking in the measure or the character of the fruit he bears. Do believe that the Word is meant to lead us on to a fuller experience of the Father's purpose of love, of Christ's fullness, and of the wonderful privilege of bearing much fruit in the salvation of men.

More fruit. The word is a most encouraging one. Let us listen to it. The message of "more fruit" only comes to the branch which is already bearing fruit. God does not demand this as Pharaoh the taskmaster, or as Moses the lawgiver, without providing the means. He comes as a Father, who gives what He asks, and works what He commands. He comes to us as the living branches of the living Vine, and offers to work the "more fruit" in us. He will do so only if we yield ourselves into His hands. Will we not admit the claim, accept the offer, and look to Him to work it in us?

"That it may bring forth more fruit." Do believe that, as the owner of a vine does everything to make the fruitage as rich and large as possible, the divine Husbandman will do all that is needed to make us bear more fruit. All He asks is that we set our heart's desire on it, entrust ourselves to His working and care, and joyfully look to Him to do His perfect work in us. God has set His heart on more fruit. Christ waits to work it in us. Let us joyfully look up to our divine Husbandman and our heavenly Vine to ensure our bearing more fruit.

Our Father which art in heaven, You are the heavenly Husbandman. And Christ is the heavenly Vine. And I am a heavenly branch, partaker of His heavenly life, to bear His heavenly fruit. Father, let the power of His life so fill me that I may always bear more fruit, to the glory of Your name.

Chapter Six

THE CLEANSING

"Every branch that beareth fruit, he purgeth it, that it may bring forth more fruit"—John 15:2.

There are two remarkable things about the vine. No other plant bears fruit which has so much spirit in it—spirit which can be abundantly distilled. And, no other plant runs so quickly into wild wood, hinders its fruit, and therefore needs the most merciless pruning. I look out of my window here on large vineyards, and see that the chief care of the vine-dresser is the pruning. You may have a trellis vine rooted so deeply in good soil that it does not need digging, manuring, or watering. But, it cannot dispense with pruning if it is to bear good fruit.

Some trees need occasional pruning. Others bear perfect fruit without any. The vine *must* have it. And so our Lord tells us, at the very beginning of the parable, that the one work the Father does to the fruit-bearing branch is "He purgeth it, that it may bring forth more fruit."

Consider for a moment what this pruning or

cleansing is. It is not the removal of weeds or thorns, or anything from without that may hinder the growth. No, it is the cutting off of the long shoots of the previous year. It is the removal of something that comes from within, that has been produced by the life of the vine itself. It is the removal of something that is a sign of the vigor of its life. The more vigorous the growth has been, the greater the need for the pruning.

The honest, healthy wood of the vine has to be cut away. And why? Because it would consume too much of the sap to fill all the long shoots of last year's growth. The sap must be saved up and used for fruit alone. The branches, sometimes eight and ten feet long, are cut down close to the stem. Nothing is left but just one or two inches of wood, enough to bear the grapes. It is only when everything that is not necessary for fruit-bearing has been relentlessly cut down, and when as little of the branches as possible remain, that full, rich fruit may be expected.

What a solemn, precious lesson! It is not to sin alone that the cleansing of the Husbandman refers to here. It refers to our own Christian activity, as it is developed in the very act of bearing fruit. It is this that must be cut down and cleansed away. We have, in working for God, to use our natural gifts of wisdom, eloquence, influence, or zeal. And yet, they are in constant danger of being unduly developed, and then trusted in. And so, after each season of work, God has to bring us to the end of ourselves. He must make us conscious of the helplessness and the danger of all that is of man. He must help us to feel that we are nothing.

All that is to remain of self is just enough to receive the power of the life-giving sap of the Holy Spirit. What is of man must be reduced to its very lowest measure. All that is inconsistent with the most entire devotion to Christ's service must be removed. The more perfect the cleansing and cutting away of all that is of self, the less there will be to interfere with the guidance of the Holy Spirit. Then, the consecration of our whole being can be more intensely and entirely at the Spirit's disposal. This is the true circumcision of the heart—the circumcision of Christ. This is the true crucifixion with Christ, bearing about the dying of the Lord Jesus in the body.

Blessed cleansing, God's own cleansing! How we may rejoice in the assurance that we will bring forth more fruit.

O our holy Husbandman, cleanse and cut away all that there is in us that could become a source of self-confidence and glorying. Lord, keep us very low, so that no flesh may glory in Your presence. We do trust You to do Your work.

Chapter Seven

THE PRUNING KNIFE

"Now ye are clean through the word which I have spoken unto you"—John 15:3.

What is the heavenly Husbandman's pruning knife? It is often said to be affliction, but is this the tool He uses? How is it that there are many who experience long seasons free from adversity? Why does it appear that there are some to whom God bestows lifelong kindness?

No, it is the Word of God that is the knife—sharper than any two-edged sword—which pierces even to the dividing asunder of the soul and spirit. It is the Word that is quick to discern the thoughts and intentions of the heart. Only when affliction leads to this discipline of the Word can it become a blessing. The lack of this heart-cleansing through the Word is the reason why affliction is so often unsanctified. Not even Paul's thorn in the flesh could become a blessing until Christ's word—"My strength is made perfect in weakness" (2 Corinthians 12:9)—had made him see the danger of self-exaltation. Only that could make him willing to rejoice in weaknesses.

The Word is God's pruning knife. Jesus says, "Ye are clean through the word which I have spoken unto you." How searchingly that word was spoken by Him. How His words were as a sharp two-edged sword as He had taught them, "Except a man deny himself, lose his life, forsake all, hate father and mother, he cannot be My disciple, he is not worthy of Me." How strong was His message as He humbled their pride, reproved their lack of love, and foretold of their all forsaking Him.

From the beginning of His ministry in the Sermon on the Mount to His words of warning on the last night, His Word had tried and cleansed them. He had discovered and condemned all there was of self. They were now emptied and cleansed, ready for the incoming of the Holy Spirit.

When the soul gives up its own thoughts of what Christianity is, and yields itself—heartily, humbly, patiently—to the teaching of the Word by the Spirit, the Father will do His blessed work. He will prune and cleanse away all of nature and self that mixes with our work and hinders His Spirit. Let those who want to know all that the Husbandman can do for them, all that the Vine can bring forth through them, seek earnestly to yield themselves entirely to the blessed cleansing through the Word. Let them, in their study of the Word, receive it as a hammer which breaks and opens up, as a fire which melts and refines, and as a sword which lays bare and slays all that is of the flesh. The word of conviction will prepare them for the word of comfort and of hope. And, the Father will cleanse them through the Word.

All who are branches of the true Vine, each time you read or hear the Word, wait on Him to use it for His cleansing of the branch. Set your heart upon His desire for more fruit. Trust Him as Husbandman to work it. Yield yourselves in simple, childlike surrender to the cleansing work of His Word and Spirit, and you may count on His purpose being fulfilled in you.

Father, cleanse me through Your Word. Let it search out and bring to light all that is of self and the flesh in my faith. Let it cut away every root of self-confidence, that the Vine may find me wholly free to receive His life and Spirit. O my holy Husbandman, I trust You to care for the branch as much as for the Vine. Only You are my hope.

Chapter Eight

ABIDE

"Abide in me, and I in you"—John 15:4.

When a new graft is placed in a vine, and it abides there, a twofold process takes place. The first is in the wood. The graft shoots its little roots and fibers down into the stem, the stem grows up into the graft, and the structural union is completed. The graft abides and becomes one with the vine. Even if the vine were to die, the graft would still be one wood with it. Then, there is the second process. The sap of the vine enters the new structure, and uses it as a passage through which sap can flow into the young shoots and leaves and fruit. Here is the vital union— into the graft which abides in the stock, the stock enters with sap to abide in it. When our Lord says, "Abide in Me, and I in you," He points to something analogous to this. "Abide in Me": that refers more to that which *we* have to do. We have to trust and obey, to detach ourselves from all else. We must reach out after Him and cling to Him, to sink ourselves into Him. As we do this—through the grace He gives—a character is formed, and a heart prepared for the fuller experience: "I in you." God strengthens us with might by the Spirit in the inner man, and Christ dwells in the heart by faith.

Many believers pray and long very earnestly for the filling of the Spirit and the indwelling of Christ. They wonder why they do not make more progress. The reason is often this, the "I in you" cannot come because the "abide in Me" is not maintained. "There is one body, and one Spirit" (Ephesians 4:4). Before the Spirit can fill, the body must be prepared. The graft must have grown into the stem, and be abiding in it, before the sap can flow through to bring forth fruit. If in lowly obedience we follow Christ, even in external things (denying ourselves, forsaking the world), and seek to be conformable to Him, and to abide in Him, then we may be able to receive and enjoy the "I in you." The work required of us: *"Abide in Me,"* will prepare us for the work undertaken by Him: *"I in you."*

In. The two parts of the commandment have their unity in that central, deep-meaning word *in.* There is no deeper word in Scripture. God is *in all.* God dwells *in* Christ. Christ lives *in* God. We are *in* Christ. Christ is *in* us: our life taken up into His; His life received into ours. In a divine reality that words cannot express, we are *in* Him and He is *in* us. And the words, "Abide in Me and I in you," just tell us to believe in this divine mystery. We are to count on our God the Husbandman, and Christ the Vine, to make it divinely true. No thinking or teaching or praying can grasp it—it is a divine mystery of love. As little as we can influence the relationship, can we understand it. Let us just look upon this infinite, divine, omnipotent Vine loving us, holding us, working in us. Let us, in the faith of His working, abide and rest in Him, ever turning heart and hope to Him alone. And let us count on Him to fulfill in us the mystery: "Ye in Me, and I in you."

Blessed Lord, You bid me to abide in You. How can I abide, Lord, except by Your showing Yourself to me, waiting to receive and welcome and keep me? I ask You to show me how You, as Vine, undertake to do all. To be occupied with You is to abide in You. Here I am, Lord, a branch, cleansed and abiding— resting in You, and awaiting the inflow of Your life and grace.

Chapter Nine

EXCEPT YE ABIDE

"As the branch cannot bear fruit of itself, except it abide in the vine; no more can ye, except ye abide in me"—John 15:4.

We all know the meaning of the word *except*. It expresses some indispensable condition, some inevitable law. "The branch cannot bear fruit of itself, *except* it abide in the vine; no more can ye, *except* ye abide in me." There is only one way for the branch to bear fruit, there is no other possibility—it must abide in unbroken communion with the vine. Not of itself, but only of the vine, does the fruit come. Christ had already said, "Abide in me." In nature, the branch teaches us the lesson so clearly.

It is such a wonderful privilege to be called and allowed to abide in the heavenly Vine. One might have thought it needless to add these words of warning. But no—Christ knows so well how much a renunciation of self this "Abide in me" implies. He knows how strong and universal the tendency would be to seek to bear fruit by our own efforts. He realizes how difficult it would be to get us to believe that actual, continuous abiding in Him is an absolute necessity! He insists upon the truth: *Not of itself* can the branch bear fruit; *except it abide,* it cannot bear fruit. "No more can ye, *except ye abide in Me."*

But must this be taken literally? Must I, as exclusively, manifestly, unceasingly, and absolutely as the branch abides in the vine, be equally given up to find my whole life in Christ alone? I must indeed. The *except ye abide* is as universal as the *except it abide.* The *no more can ye* allows no exception or modification. If I am to be a true branch, if I am to bear fruit, and if I am to be what Christ as Vine wants me to be, my whole existence must be as exclusively devoted to abiding in Him as the natural branch is to abiding in its vine.

Let me learn the lesson. Abiding is to be an act of the will and the whole heart. Just as there are degrees in seeking and serving God, "not with a perfect heart" (2 Chronicles 25:2), or "with the whole heart" (Psalm 119:2), so there may be degrees in abiding. In regeneration, the divine life enters us. But, it does not all at once master and fill our whole being. This comes as a matter of command and obedience.

There is unspeakable danger of our not giving ourselves with our whole heart to abide. There is unspeakable danger of our giving ourselves to work for God—to bear fruit—but doing so with little of the true abiding, the wholehearted losing of ourselves in Christ and His life. There is unspeakable danger of much work, but little fruit, for lack of this vital relationship. We must allow the words, "not of itself," "except it abide," to do their work of searching and exposing. They must prune and cleanse all that there is of self-will and self-confidence in our life. This will deliver us from this great evil, and so prepare us for His teaching, giving the full meaning of the word in us: "Abide in me, and I in you."

Our blessed Lord desires to call us away from ourselves and our own strength, and draw us to Himself and His strength. Let us accept the warning, and turn with great fear and self-distrust to Him to do His work. "Our life is hid with Christ in God" (Colossians 3:3)! That life is a heavenly mystery, hid from the wise even among Christians, and revealed to the babes. The childlike spirit learns that life is given from heaven every day and every moment to the soul that accepts the teaching: "Not of itself," "Except it abide," and seeks its all in the Vine. Abiding in the Vine then comes to be nothing more nor less than the restful surrender of the soul to let Christ have all and work all—as completely as in nature, the branch knows and seeks nothing but the vine.

Abide in Me. I have heard, my Lord, that with every command You also give the power to obey. With Your "rise and walk," the lame man leaped. I accept Your word, "Abide in me," as a word of power, that gives power. Even now I say, Yea, Lord, I will, I do abide in You.

Chapter Ten

I AM THE VINE

"I am the vine, ye are the branches"—John 15:5.

In the previous verse, Christ said, "Abide in Me." He then announced the great, unalterable law of all branch-life, on earth or in heaven, *"not of itself"*: *"except it abide."* In the opening words of the parable, He has already spoken, **"I am the true vine."** He now repeats the words. He wants us to understand— note well the lesson, simple as it appears, it is the key to the abiding life—that the only way to obey the command, **"Abide in me,"** is to have our eyes and heart fixed on Him.

"Abide in Me...I am the true vine." Yes, study this holy mystery until you see Christ as the true Vine, bearing, strengthening, supplying, and inspiring all His branches. He will *be and do in each branch all that it needs,* and the abiding will come of itself.

Yes, gaze upon Him as the true Vine, until you feel what a heavenly mystery it is, and are compelled to ask the Father to reveal it to you by His Holy Spirit.

He to whom God reveals the glory of the true Vine—
he who sees what Jesus is and waits to do every
moment—can do nothing but abide. The vision of
Christ is an irresistible attraction; it draws and holds
us like a magnet. Listen continually to the living
Christ still speaking to you, and waiting to show you
the meaning and power of His Word: *"I am the
vine."*

How much weary labor is involved in striving to
understand what abiding is! How much fruitless
effort goes along with trying to attain it! Why is this?
Because the attention is turned to the abiding as a
work we have to do, instead of the living Christ, in
whom we have to abide. He is Himself to hold and
keep us. We think of abiding as a continual strain
and effort—we forget that it means rest from effort
to one who has found the place of his abode.

Do notice how Christ said, "Abide *in Me.* I am the
Vine that brings forth and holds and strengthens and
makes fruitful the branches. Abide in Me, rest in
Me, and let Me do My work. I am the true Vine. All I
am and speak and do is divine truth, giving the
actual reality of what is said. I am the Vine, only
consent and yield your all to Me. I will do all in you."

And sometimes it happens that souls who have
never been especially occupied with the thought of
abiding, abide all the time, because they are occupied with Christ. Not that the word *abide* is not
important. Christ used it so often because it is the
very key to the Christian life. But He wants us to
understand it in its true sense—"Come out of every

other place, and every other trust and occupation; come out of self with its reasoning and efforts; come and rest in what I will do. Live out of yourself; abide in *Me*. Know that you are *in Me*; you need no more. Remain there *in Me.*"

"I am the vine." Christ did not keep this mystery hidden from His disciples. He revealed it—first in words here, then in power when the Holy Spirit came down. He will reveal it to us, too—first in the thoughts and confessions and desires these words awaken, then in power by the Spirit. Do let us wait on Him to show us all the heavenly meaning of the mystery. Let our chief thought and aim each day in our quiet time—in the inner chamber with Him and His Word—be to get the heart fixed on Him. Let us be assured that all a vine can ever do for its branches, my Lord Jesus will do—is doing—for me. Give Him time. Give Him your ear, that He may whisper and explain the divine secret: "I am the vine."

Above all, remember, Christ is the Vine of God's planting, and you are a branch of *God's grafting. Stand always before God, in Christ*—waiting for all grace from God, *in Christ*. Yielding yourself to bear the "more fruit" the Husbandman asks, *in Christ*. And pray much for the revelation of the mystery that all the love and power of God which rested on Christ is working in you, too. "I am God's Vine," Jesus says, "All I am I have from Him; all I am is for you; God will work it in you."

I am the Vine. Blessed Lord, speak that word into

my soul. Then, I will know that all Your fullness is for me. And, I can count on You to stream it into me. My abiding is so easy and so sure when I forget and lose myself in the adoring faith that the Vine holds the branch and supplies its every need.

Chapter Eleven

YE ARE THE BRANCHES

"I am the vine, ye are the branches"—John 15:5.

Christ has already said much about the branch. In this verse, He makes a personal application: "Ye are the branches of whom I have been speaking. As I am the Vine, engaged to be and do all the branches need, so I now ask you, through the Holy Spirit whom I have been promising you, to accept the place I give you, and to be My branches on earth."

The relationship He seeks to establish is an intensely personal one. It all hinges on the two little words *I* and *you*. And, it is as intensely personal for us as it was for the first disciples. Let us present ourselves before our Lord, until He speaks to each of us in power, and our whole soul feels it: I am the Vine; you are the branch.

Dear disciples of Jesus, however young or feeble, hear the voice, "Ye are the branches." You must be *nothing less.* Let no false humility, no carnal fear of sacrifice, no unbelieving doubts as to what you feel able to do, keep you from saying, "I will be a branch,

40

with all that may mean—a branch, very feeble, but yet as like the Vine as I can be, for I am of the same nature, and receive of the same Spirit. I will be a branch, utterly helpless, and yet just as manifestly set apart before God and men. I will be as wholly given up to the work of bearing fruit as the Vine itself. I will be a branch, nothing in myself, and yet resting and rejoicing in the faith which knows that He will provide for all. Yes, by His grace, I will be nothing less than a branch, and all He means it to be, that through me, He may bring forth His fruit."

You are the branch. You need be *nothing more.* You need not for one single moment of the day take upon yourself the responsibility of the Vine. You need not leave the place of entire dependence and unbounded confidence. You need, least of all, to be anxious as to how you are to understand the mystery, fulfill its conditions, or work out its blessed aim. The Vine will give all and work all. The Father—the Husbandman—watches over your union with and growth in the Vine. You need be nothing more than a branch. Only a branch! Let that be your watchword. It will lead you in the path of continual surrender to Christ's working. You will walk with true obedience to His every command and joyful expectancy of all His grace.

Is there anyone who now asks, "How can I learn to say this correctly, 'Only a branch!' and to live it out?" Dear soul, the character of a branch, its strength, and the fruit it bears, depend entirely upon the Vine. And your life as a branch depends entirely

41

upon your comprehension of what our Lord Jesus is. Therefore, never separate the two words, "I the Vine—you the branch." Your life and strength and fruit depend on what your Lord Jesus is! Therefore, worship and trust Him. Let Him be your one desire and the one occupation of your heart.

When you feel that you do not and cannot know Him correctly, just remember it is a part of His responsibility as Vine to make Himself known to you. He does this not in thoughts and conceptions— no—but in a hidden growth within the life that is humbly, restfully, and entirely given up to wait on Him. The Vine reveals itself within the branch— thence comes the growth and fruit. Christ dwells and works within His branch. Only be a branch, waiting on Him to do all. He will be to You the true Vine. The Father Himself, the divine Husbandman, is able to make you a branch worthy of the heavenly Vine. You will not be disappointed.

Ye are the branches. This word, too, Lord! O speak it in power unto my soul. Do not let the branch of the earthly vine put me to shame, but as it only lives to bear the fruit of the vine, may my life on earth have no other wish or aim but to let You bring forth fruit through me.

Chapter Twelve

MUCH FRUIT

"He that abideth in me, and I in him, the same bringeth forth much fruit"—John 15:5.

Our Lord has spoken of fruit, more fruit. He now adds the thought: much fruit. There is in the Vine such fullness—the care of the divine Husbandman is so sure of success—that the much fruit is not a demand. It is the simple promise of what must come to the branch that lives in the double abiding—he in Christ, and Christ in him. "The same bringeth forth much fruit." It is certain.

Have you ever noticed the difference, in the Christian life, between work and fruit? A machine can do work: only life can bear fruit. A law can compel work: only love can spontaneously bring forth fruit. Work implies effort and labor: the essential idea of fruit is that it is the silent, natural, restful produce of our inner life. The gardener may labor to give his apple tree the digging and manuring, the watering and the pruning it needs. But, he can do nothing to produce the apple. The tree bears its own fruit. Likewise, in the Christian life, "The fruit of the

Spirit is love, joy, peace..." (Galatians 5:22). The healthy life bears much fruit.

The connection between work and fruit is perhaps best seen in the expression, "fruitful in every good work" (Colossians 1:10). It is only when good works come as the fruit of the indwelling Spirit that they are acceptable to God. Under the compulsion of law and conscience, or the influence of inclination and zeal, men may be most diligent in good works. And yet, they find that they have little spiritual result. There can be no reason except this—their works are man's effort, instead of being the fruit of the Spirit. They do not know the restful, natural outcome of the Spirit's operation within them.

Let all workers come and listen to our holy Vine as He reveals the law of sure and abundant fruitfulness, "He that abideth in me, and I in him, the same bringeth forth much fruit." The gardener cares for one thing—the strength and healthy life of his tree. The fruit follows of itself. If you want to bear fruit, see that the inner life is perfectly right, that your relationship to Christ Jesus is clear and close. Begin each day with Him in the morning, to know in truth that you are abiding in Him and He in you. Christ tells us that nothing less will do. It is not your willing and running, it is not by your might or strength, but—"by my Spirit, saith the Lord" (Zechariah 4:6). Meet each new engagement, undertake every new work, with your ears and heart open to the Master's voice, "He that abideth in me...beareth much fruit." You see to the abiding; He will see to the fruit, for He will give it in you and through you.

O my brethren, it is Christ who must do all! The Vine provides the sap, the life, and the strength. The branch waits, rests, receives, and bears the fruit. Oh, the blessedness of being only branches, through whom the Spirit flows and brings God's life to men!

I pray you, take time and ask the Holy Spirit to help you to realize the unspeakably solemn place you occupy in the mind of God. He has planted you into His Son with the calling and the power to bear *much fruit*. Accept that place. Look always to God, and to Christ, and joyfully expect to be what God has planned to make you—a fruitful branch.

Much fruit! So be it, blessed Lord Jesus. It can be, for You are the Vine. It will be, for I am abiding in You. It must be, for Your Father is the Husbandman who cleanses the branch. Yes, much fruit, out of the abundance of Your grace.

Chapter Thirteen

YE CAN DO NOTHING

"Apart from Me ye can do nothing"—John 15:5.

In everything, the life of the branch is to be the exact counterpart of that of the Vine. Of Himself, Jesus had said, "The Son can do nothing of himself" (John 5:19). As the outcome of that entire dependence, He could add, "For what things soever he doeth, these also doeth the Son likewise" (John 5:19). As Son, He did not receive His life from the Father once and for all, but moment by moment. His life was a continual waiting on the Father for all He was to do. And so Christ says of His disciples, "Apart from me ye can do nothing." He means it literally.

To everyone who wants to live the true disciple life—to bring forth fruit and glorify God—this message comes: You can do nothing. What has been said, "He that abideth in me, and I in him, the same beareth much fruit," is here enforced by the simplest and strongest of arguments, "Abiding in Me is indispensable, for, of yourselves, you can do nothing to maintain or act out the heavenly life."

A deep conviction of the truth of this word lies at the very root of a strong spiritual life. As little as I created myself, as little as I could raise a man from the dead, can I give myself the divine life. As little as I can give it myself, can I maintain or increase it.

Every motion is the work of God through Christ and His Spirit. It is as a man believes this that he will take up that position of entire and continual dependence which is the very essence of the life of faith. With the spiritual eye, he sees Christ continually supplying grace for every breathing and deepening of the spiritual life. His whole heart says Amen to the word, *You can do nothing.* And just because he does so, he can also say, "I can do all things through Christ which strengtheneth me" (Philippians 4:13). The sense of helplessness, and the abiding to which it compels, leads to true fruitfulness and diligence in good works.

Apart from Me ye can do nothing. What a plea and what a call to abide in Christ every moment! We have only to go back to the vine to see how true it is. Look again at that little branch, utterly helpless and fruitless except as it receives sap from the vine. Learn that the full conviction of not being able to do anything apart from Christ is just what you need to teach you to abide in your heavenly Vine. It is this that is the great meaning of the pruning which Christ spoke of. All that is of self must be brought low, that our confidence may be in Christ alone. "Abide in Me"—much fruit! "Apart from Me"—nothing! Is there any doubt as to what our choice should be?

The one lesson of the parable is—as surely, as naturally, as the branch abides in the vine, *You can abide in Christ.* For in this, He is the true Vine, God is the Husbandman, and you are a branch. Will we not cry to God to deliver us forever from the "apart from Me," and to make the "abide in Me" an unceasing reality? Let your heart go out to what Christ is, and can do. Receive His divine power and His tender love for each of His branches, and you will say with increasing confidence, "Lord! I am abiding. I will bear much fruit. My weakness is my strength. So be it. Apart from You, nothing. In You, much fruit."

Apart from Me—you are nothing. Lord, I gladly accept the arrangement: I am nothing—You are all. My nothingness is my highest blessing, because You are the Vine, which gives and works all. So be it, Lord! I am nothing, ever waiting on Your fullness. Lord, reveal to me the glory of this blessed life.

Chapter Fourteen

WITHERED BRANCHES

"If a man abide not in me, he is cast forth as a branch, and is withered; and men gather them, and cast them into the fire, and they are burned"—John 15:6.

The lessons these words teach are very simple and solemn. A man may believe he has a relationship with Christ—he may count himself to be in Him—and yet he can be cast forth. There is such a thing as not abiding in Christ, which leads to withering up and burning. There is such a thing as a withered branch. It is one in whom the initial union with Christ appears to have taken place, and yet it seems that his faith was only for a time. What a solemn call to look around and see if there are withered branches in our churches—to look within and see whether we are indeed abiding and bearing fruit!

And what may be the cause of this "not abiding"? With some, it is that they never understood how the Christian calling leads to holy obedience and loving service. They were content with the thought that they had believed, and were safe from hell. They had neither the motive nor the power to abide in Christ—they did not know the need of it. With others, it was that the cares of the world, or its prosperity, choked the Word. They had never forsaken all to follow Christ. With still others, it was that their religion and their faith was in the wisdom of men, and not in the power of God. They trusted in the means of grace, in their own sincerity, or in the soundness of their faith in justifying grace. They had never even come to seek an entire abiding in Christ as their only safety. No wonder that, when the hot winds of temptation or persecution blew, they withered away. They were not truly rooted in Christ.

Let us open our eyes and see if there are withered branches in our churches. Look for young believers, whose confessions were once bright, but who are growing cold. Search out old members, who have retained their profession, but have lost the life that once appeared to be there. Let ministers and believers take Christ's words to heart, and ask the Lord whether there is anything to be done for branches that are beginning to wither. And let the word *Abide* ring through the Church until every believer has caught it—there is no safety without a true abiding in Christ.

Let each of us turn within. Is our life fresh, green, and vigorous, bringing forth its fruit in its season? (See Psalm 1:3; 92:13,14; Jeremiah 17:7,8.) Let us accept every warning with a willing mind, and let Christ's "if a man abide not" give new urgency to His "abide in me." To the upright soul, the secret of abiding will become ever simpler—just the consciousness of the place in which He has put me. It will be the childlike resting in my union with Him, and the trustful assurance that He will keep me. Oh, do let us believe there is a life that knows of no withering, that is ever green, and that brings forth fruit abundantly!

Withered! O my Father, watch over me, keep me, and let nothing ever for a moment hinder the freshness that comes from a full abiding in the Vine. Let the very thought of a withered branch fill me with holy fear and watchfulness.

Chapter Fifteen

WHAT YE WILL

"If ye abide in me, and my words abide in you, ye shall ask what ye will, and it shall be done unto you"—John 15:7.

The whole existence of the branch in the vine is one of unceasing prayer. Without intermission, it is ever calling, "O my vine, send the sap I need to bear your fruit." And its prayers are never unanswered. It asks what it needs, what it will, and it is done.

The healthy life of the believer in Christ is equally one of unceasing prayer. Consciously or unconsciously, he lives in continual dependence. The word of his Lord, "You can do nothing," has taught him that his asking and receiving must be as unbroken as the continuance of the branch in the vine. The promise of our text gives us infinite boldness, "Ask what ye will, and it shall be done unto you."

The promise is given in direct connection with fruit-bearing. Limit it to yourself and your own needs, and you rob it of its power. You rob yourself of the power of appropriating it. Christ was sending these disciples out, and they were ready to give their life for the world. To them, He gave the disposal of the treasures of heaven. Their prayers would bring the Spirit and the power they needed for their work.

The promise is given in direct connection with the coming of the Spirit. The Spirit is mentioned in the parable as seldom as the sap of the vine is mentioned. But, both are referred to throughout. In the chapter preceding the parable, our Lord had spoken of the Holy Spirit. The Spirit is referred to in connection with their inner life, being in them, and revealing Himself within them (John 14:15-23).

In the next chapter, He speaks of the Holy Spirit in connection with their work, coming to them, convincing the world, and glorifying Him (John 16:7-14). To avail ourselves of the unlimited prayer promises, we must be men who are filled with the Spirit, and wholly given up to the work and glory of Jesus. The Spirit will lead us into the truth of its meaning and the certainty of its fulfillment.

Let us realize that we can only fulfill our calling to bear much fruit by praying much. In Christ are hid all the treasures men around us need. In Him, all God's children are blessed with all spiritual blessings. He is full of grace and truth. But, prayer, much prayer, strong believing prayer, is needed to bring about these blessings. And let us equally remember that we cannot appropriate the promise without first living a life given up for men. Many try to take the promise, and then look around for what they can ask. This is not the way, but the very opposite. Get the heart burdened with the need of souls, and the command and power to save them will come to claim the promise.

Let us claim it as one of the revelations of our wonderful life in the Vine: He tells us that if we ask in His name, in virtue of our union with Him, whatever it is, it will be done to us. Souls are perishing because there is too little prayer. God's children are feeble because there is too little prayer. We bear so little fruit because there is so little prayer. The faith of this promise would make us strong to pray. Let us not rest until it has entered into our very heart, and drawn us in the power of Christ to continue, labor, and strive in prayer until the blessing comes in power. To be a branch means not only bearing fruit on earth, but power in prayer to bring forth blessings from heaven. Abiding fully means praying much.

Ask what ye will. O my Lord, why is it that our hearts are so little able to accept these words in their divine simplicity? Oh, help me to see that we need nothing less than this promise to overcome the powers of the world and Satan! Teach us to pray in the faith of this Your promise.

Chapter Sixteen

IF YE ABIDE

"If ye abide in me, and my words abide in you, ye shall ask what ye will, and it shall be done unto you"—John 15:7.

The reason the Vine and its branches are such a true parable of the Christian life is that all nature has one source, and breathes one spirit. The plant world was created to be an object lesson to man. It was to teach him his entire dependence on God, and his security in that dependence. He who clothes the lilies will much more clothe us. He who gives the trees and the vines their beauty and their fruits, making each what He meant it to be, will much more certainly make us what He would have us to be.

The only difference is, what God works in the trees is by a power of which they are not conscious. He wants to work in us with our consent. This is the nobility of man—he has a will which can co-operate with God in understanding, approving, and accepting what He offers to do.

If ye abide. Here is the difference between the

branch of the natural and the branch of the spiritual Vine. The former abides by force of nature. The latter abides, not by force of will, but by a divine power given to the consent of the will. Such is the wonderful provision which God has made. What the power of nature does in the one case, the power of grace will do in the other. The branch can abide in the Vine.

If ye abide in Me...ask what ye will. If we are to live a true prayer life, with the love, power, and experience of prayer marking it, there must be no question about the abiding. And if we abide, there need be no question about the liberty of asking what we will. There need be no doubt about the certainty of its being done. There is the one condition: "If ye abide in me." There must be no hesitation about the possibility or the certainty of it. We must gaze on that little branch and its wonderful power of bearing such beautiful fruit until we truly learn to abide.

And what is its secret? Be wholly occupied with Jesus. Sink the roots of your faith, love, and obedience deep down into Him. Come away out of every other place to abide there. Give up everything for the inconceivable privilege of being a branch of the glorified Son of God in heaven. Let Christ be first. Let Christ be all. Do not be occupied with the abiding—be occupied with Christ. He will hold you; He will keep you abiding in Him. He will abide in you.

If ye abide in Me, and My words abide in you. This He gives as the equivalent of the other expression: "I in you. If my words abide in You." That is, abide not only in meditation, memory, love, and faith—all these are needed—but above all, abide in obedience. If these words enter into your will, your being, and constitute your life—if they transform your character into their own likeness, and you become and are what they speak and mean—ask what you will; it will be done unto you. Your words to God in prayer will be the fruit of Christ and His words living in you.

Ask what ye will, and it shall be done unto you. Believe in the truth of this promise. Set yourself to be an intercessor for men. Be a fruit-bearing intercessor, always calling forth more blessing. Such faith and prayer will wonderfully help you to abide wholly and unceasingly.

If ye abide. Yes, Lord, the power to pray and the power to prevail must depend on this abiding in You. As You are the Vine, You are the divine Intercessor, who breathes Your Spirit in us. Oh, for the grace to abide simply and wholly in You, and ask great things!

Chapter Seventeen

THE FATHER GLORIFIED

"Herein is my Father glorified, that ye bear much fruit"—John 15:8.

How can we glorify God? Not by adding to His glory or bringing Him any new glory that He has not. But simply by allowing His glory to shine out through us. By simply yielding ourselves to Him, so that His glory may manifest itself in us and through us to the world. In a vineyard or a vine bearing much fruit, the owner is glorified, as it tells of his skill and care. In the disciple who bears much fruit, the Father is glorified. Before men and angels, proof is given of the glory of God's grace and power. God's glory shines out through him.

This is what Peter means when he writes: "If any man minister, let him do it as of the ability which God giveth: that God in all things may be glorified through Jesus Christ" (1 Peter 4:11). As a man works and serves in a power which comes from God alone, God gets all the glory. When we confess that the ability came from God alone, he who does the work, and they who see it, equally glorify God. It was God who did it. Men judge by the fruit of a garden the worth of the gardener. Men judge God by the fruit that the branches of the Vine of His planting bear. Little fruit brings little glory to God. It brings no honor to either the Vine or the Husbandman. "Herein is My Father glorified, that ye bear much fruit."

We have sometimes mourned our lack of fruit—a loss to ourselves and our fellow men—and blame it on our feebleness. Let us rather think of the sin and shame of little fruit as robbing God of the glory He ought to get from us. Let us learn the secret of bringing glory to God—serving with the ability which God gave us. The full acceptance of Christ's word, "You can do nothing"; the simple faith in God, who works all in all; the abiding in Christ through whom the divine Husbandman does His work and gets much fruit—this is the life that will bring glory to God.

Much fruit. God asks it; see that you give it. God can be content with nothing less; you be content with nothing less. Let these words of Christ—fruit, more fruit, much fruit—abide in you until you think as He does. Be prepared to take from Him, the heavenly Vine, what He has for you. Much fruit: herein is My Father glorified. Let the very height of the demand be your encouragement. It is so entirely beyond your power that it throws you more entirely upon Christ, your true Vine. He can, He will, make it true in you.

Much fruit. God asks because He needs. He does

not ask fruit from the branches of His Vine for show—to prove what He can do. No, He needs it for the salvation of men. It is in this way that He is to be glorified. Throw yourself in much prayer on your Vine and your Husbandman. Cry to God and your Father to give you fruit to bring to men. Take the burden of the hungry and the perishing on you, as Jesus did when He was moved with compassion. Then, your power in prayer, your abiding, and your bearing much fruit to the glory of the Father will have a reality and a certainty you never knew before.

The Father glorified. Blessed prospect—God glorifying Himself in me, showing forth the glory of His goodness and power in what He works in me, and through me. What a motive to bear much fruit, just as much as He works in me! Father, glorify Yourself in me.

Chapter Eighteen

TRUE DISCIPLES

"Herein is my Father glorified, that ye bear much fruit, so shall ye be my disciples"—John 15:8.

And, are those who do not bear much fruit not disciples? They may be, but in a backward and immature stage. Of those who bear much fruit, Christ says, in effect, "These are My disciples, such as I would have them be—these are true disciples." We say about someone in whom the idea of manliness is realized: That is a man! Likewise, our Lord reveals who are disciples after His heart, worthy of the name: Those who bear much fruit.

We find this double sense of the word *disciple* in the Gospel. Sometimes, it is applied to all who accept Christ's teaching. At other times, it includes only the inner circle of those who followed Christ wholly, and gave themselves to His training for service. The difference has existed throughout all ages. There have always been a smaller number of God's people who have sought to serve Him with their whole heart, while the majority have been content with a very small amount of the knowledge of His grace and will.

And what is the difference between this smaller inner circle and the many who do not seek admission to it? We find it in the words: *much fruit.* With many Christians, the thought of personal safety—at first, a legitimate reason to believe—remains throughout life as the one aim of their faith in God. The idea of service and fruit is always a secondary and very subordinate thought. The honest longing for much fruit does not trouble them. Souls that have heard the call to live wholly for their Lord—to give their life for Him as He gave His for them—can never be satisfied with this. Their cry is to bear as much fruit as they possible can, as much as their Lord can ever desire or give through them.

Bear much fruit; so shall ye be My disciples. I beg every reader to consider these words most seriously. Do not be content with the thought of gradually doing a little more or better work. In this way it may never come. Take the words, *much fruit,* as the promise which your heavenly Vine reveals about what you must and can be. Fully accept the impossibility—the utter folly—of attempting it in your own strength. Let the words call you to look on the Vine anew, and undertake to live out their heavenly fullness in you. Let them waken in you once again the faith and the confession, "I am a branch of the true Vine. I can bear much fruit to His glory, and the glory of the Father."

We need not judge others. But, we see in God's

Word everywhere that there are two classes of disciples. Let there be no hesitation as to where we take our place. Let us ask Him to reveal to us how He asks and claims a life which is wholly given up to Him. Let us ask to be as full of His Spirit as He can make us. Let our desire be nothing less than perfect cleansing, unbroken abiding, closest communion, abundant fruitfulness—*true* branches of the true Vine.

The world is perishing; the Church is failing; Christ's cause is suffering. Christ is grieving on account of the lack of wholehearted Christians bearing much fruit. Though you hardly see what it implies or how it is to come, say to Him that you are His branch to bear much fruit. Tell Him that you are ready to be His disciple in His own meaning of the word.

My disciples. Blessed Lord, much fruit is the proof that You, the true Vine, have in me a true branch—a disciple wholly at Your disposal. Give me, I pray, the childlike consciousness that my fruit is pleasing to You, what You count as much fruit.

Chapter Nineteen

THE WONDERFUL LOVE

"As the Father hath loved me, so have I loved you"—John 15:9.

Here, Christ leaves the parable language, and speaks plainly out of the Father. As much as the parable could teach, it could not teach the lesson of love. All that the vine does for the branch it does under the compulsion of a law of nature. There is no personal, living love to the branch. We are in danger of looking to Christ as a Savior and a supplier of every need, without any sense of the intensity of personal affection in which Christ embraces us. He is appointed by God, accepted and trusted by us, and only through Him can we find true happiness. Christ seeks to point us to this.

And how does He do so? He leads us once again to Himself, to show us how identical His own life is with ours. Even as the Father loved Him, He loves us. His life as a vine dependent on the Father was a life in the Father's love. That love was His strength and His joy. In the power of that divine love resting on Him, He lived and died. If we are to live like Him, as branches to be truly like our Vine, we must share in this, too. *Our life must have its breath and being in a heavenly love as much as His.* What the Father's love was to Him, His love will be to us. If that love made Him the true Vine, His love can make us true branches. "As the Father hath loved me, so have I loved you."

As the Father hath loved Me. And how did the Father love Him? The infinite desire and delight of God to communicate to the Son all He had Himself—to take the Son into the most complete equality with Himself, to live in the Son and have the Son live in Him—was God's love to Christ. We cannot conceive of this mystery of glory. We can only bow and worship as we try to think of it. And with such a love—with this very same love—Christ longs to communicate to us all He is and has. He desires to make us partakers of His own nature and blessedness. His delight is to live in us and have us live in Him.

And now, if Christ loves us with such an intense, infinite, divine love, what is it that hinders it from triumphing over every obstacle and getting full possession of us? The answer is simple. Even as the love of the Father to Christ is a divine mystery, so His love to us is too high for us to comprehend or attain to by any effort of our own. It is only the Holy Spirit who can continually shed abroad and reveal—in its all-conquering power—this wonderful love of God in Christ. It is the vine itself that must give the branch its growth and fruit by sending up its sap. It is Christ Himself who must, by His Holy Spirit, dwell in the heart. Then, we will know and have in us the love that passes knowledge.

As the Father hath loved Me, so have I loved you. Will we not draw near to trust, and yield to the personal, living Christ, so that He may work this love in us? Just as He knew and rejoiced every hour—the Father loveth Me—we, too, may live in the unceasing consciousness—as the Father loved Him, so He loves me.

As the Father hath loved Me, so have I loved you. Dear Lord, I am only beginning to understand how exactly the life of the Vine is to be that of the branch, too. You are the Vine, because the Father loved You, and poured His love through You. And so You love me, and my life as a branch is to be like Yours— a receiving and a giving out of heavenly love.

Chapter Twenty

ABIDE IN MY LOVE

"As the Father hath loved me, so have I loved you: abide ye in my love"—John 15:9.

Abide in My love. We speak of a man's home as his abode. Our abode, the home of our soul is to be the love of Christ. We are to live our life there, to be at home there all the day. This is what Christ means for our life to be. And, only He can truly make it so. Our continuous abiding in the Vine is to be an abiding in His love.

You have probably heard or read of what is called the higher or deeper life. It is also referred to as the richer, fuller, or more abundant life. And possibly some have told you about a wonderful change in their lives. Once a continual failure and stumbling, their lives were changed into a very blessed experience of being kept and strengthened and made exceedingly glad. If you asked them how this great blessing came to them, many would tell you it was simply this: they were led to believe that abiding in Christ's love was meant to be a reality; they were willing to give up everything for it, and then were enabled to trust Christ to make it happen.

The love of the Father to the Son is not a sentiment—it is a divine life, an infinite energy, an irresistible power. It carried Christ through life and death and the grave. The Father loved Him, dwelt in Him, and did all for Him. So the love of Christ to us is an infinite, living power that will work in us all He delights to give. The weakness in our Christian life is that we do not take time to believe that this divine love really does delight in us. It will truly possess and work all in us. We do not take time to look at the Vine bearing the branch so entirely, working all in it so completely. We strive to do for ourselves what Christ alone can—what Christ so lovingly longs to do for us.

This is the secret of the change we spoke of. It is the beginning of a new life, when the soul sees this infinite love willing to do all, and gives itself up to it. "Abide ye in my love." In believing that, it is possible to live moment by moment—knowing that everything which makes life difficult or impossible will be overcome by Christ Himself. To believe that divine love really means an infinite longing to give itself wholly to us and never leave us, and to, in faith, cast ourselves on Christ to work it in us, is the secret of the true Christian life.

And how do we acquire this faith? Turn away from the visible if you want to see and possess the invisible. Take more time with Jesus, gazing on Him as the heavenly Vine, living in the love of the Father, who wants you to live in His love. Turn away from yourself, your efforts, and your faith, if you want your heart to be filled with Him and the certainty of His love. Abiding means leaving everything else in order to occupy one place and stay there. Come away from all else, and set your heart on Jesus and His love. That love will awaken your faith and strengthen it. Occupy yourself with that love; worship it; wait for it. You may be sure it will reach out to you, and by its power take you up into itself as your abode and your home.

Abide in My love. Lord Jesus, I see it, it was Your abiding in Your Father's love that made You the true Vine, with Your divine fullness of love and blessing for us. Oh, that I may even so, as a branch, abide in Your love, for its fullness to fill me and overflow on all around.

Chapter Twenty-One

OBEY AND ABIDE

"If ye keep my commandments, ye shall abide in my love"—John 15:10.

In our previous meditation, reference was made to the entrance into a life of rest and strength. This life has often come through a true insight into the personal love of Christ, and the assurance that love indeed meant that He would keep the soul. In connection with that transition, and the faith that sees and accepts it, the word *surrender* or *consecration* is frequently used. The soul realizes that it cannot claim the keeping of this wonderful love unless it yields itself to a life of entire obedience. It also knows that the faith which can trust Christ to keep it from sinning must prove its sincerity by venturing to trust Him for the strength to obey. In that faith, it dares to give up and cut off everything that has hitherto hindered it. It promises and expects to live a life that is well pleasing to God.

This is the thought we have here in our Savior's teaching. After having spoken of a life in His love as a necessity—because it is at once a possibility and an obligation—He states what its one condition is: *"If ye keep my commandments, ye shall abide in My love."* This is surely not meant to close the door to the abode of His love which He had just opened up. It does not even approach the suggestion, which some are too ready to entertain, that as we cannot keep His commandments, we cannot abide in His love. No, "Abide in My love" is a promise.

And so, the instruction as to the way through this open door points to an attainable ideal. The love that invites to her blessed abode reaches out her hand, and enables us to keep the commandments. Do not fear. In the strength of your ascended Lord, take the vow of obedience, and give yourself to the keeping of His commandments. Through His will, loved and done, lies the path to His love.

Only let us understand what it means. It refers to our performance of all that we know to be God's will. There may be doubtful things, about which we are not sure. A sin of ignorance still has the nature of sin in it. There may be involuntary sins, which rise up in the flesh, that we cannot control or overcome. God will deal with these in due time, in the way of searching and humbling. And, if we are simple and faithful, He will give us a larger deliverance than we dare to expect.

But, all this may only be found in a truly obedient soul. Obedience refers to keeping the commandments of our Lord, and performing His will in everything in which we know it. This is a possible degree of grace. Here, Christ is speaking of our accepting obedience as the purpose of our heart. Faith in

Christ as our Vine, in His enabling and sanctifying strength and power, prepares us for this obedience of faith. It secures a life of abiding in His love.

If ye keep My commandments, ye shall abide in My love. It is the heavenly Vine unfolding the mystery of the life He gives. To those abiding in Him, He opens up the secret of the full abiding in His love. *It is the wholehearted surrender in everything to do His will that gives access to a life in the abiding enjoyment of His love.*

Obey and abide. Gracious Lord, teach me this lesson, that it is only through knowing Your will that one can know Your heart. Only through doing that will can one abide in Your love. Lord, teach me that as worthless as is the doing in my own strength, so essential and absolutely indispensable is the doing of faith in Your strength, if I want to abide in Your love.

Chapter Twenty-Two

YE, EVEN AS I

"If ye keep my commandments, ye shall abide in my love; even as I have kept my Father's commandments, and abide in his love"—John 15:10.

We have had more than one occasion to speak of the perfect similarity of the vine and the branch in nature, and in Scripture. Here, Christ no longer speaks in a parable, but tells us plainly of how His own life is the exact model of ours. He had said that it is by obedience alone that we can abide in His love. He now explains that this was the way in which He abode in the Father's love. As the Vine, so the branch. His life and strength and joy had been in the love of the Father. It was only by obedience that He abode in it. We may find our life and strength and joy in His love all the day. But, it is only by an obedience like His that we can abide in it. Perfect conformity to the Vine is one of the most precious of the lessons of the branch. It was by obedience that Christ as the Vine honored the Father as the Husbandman. It is by obedience that the believer as the branch honors Christ as the Vine.

Obey and abide. That was the law of Christ's life as much as it is to be that of ours. He was made like us in all things, so that we might be like Him in all things. He opened up a path in which we may walk even as He walked. He took our human nature to teach us how to wear it. He showed us how obedience—the first duty of man—is the only way to abide in the favor of God and enter into His glory. And now He comes to instruct and encourage us. He asks us to keep His commandments, even as He kept His Father's commandments and abides in His love.

The divine fitness of this connection between obeying and abiding, between God's commandments and His love, is easily seen. God's will is the very center of His divine perfection. As revealed in His commandments, it opens up the way for man to grow into the likeness of his Creator. In accepting and doing His will, I rise into fellowship with Him. Therefore, the Son, when coming into the world, spoke, "I come to do thy will, O God" (Hebrews 10:9). This is the place and the blessedness of man. This is what he lost in the Fall. This is what Christ came to restore. This is what, as the heavenly Vine, He asks of us and imparts to us. Even as He by keeping His Father's commandments abode in His love, we should keep His commandments and abide in His love.

Ye, even as I. The branch cannot bear fruit unless it has exactly the same life as the Vine. Our life is to be the exact counterpart of Christ's life. It can be, in the same measure as we believe in Him as the Vine, imparting Himself and His life to His branches. "Ye, even as I," the Vine says; one law, one nature, one fruit. Let us learn His lesson of obedience as the secret of abiding. Let us confess that simple, implicit, universal obedience has not had the place it should have. Christ died for us as enemies when we were disobedient. He took us up into His love. Now that we are in Him, His word is: "Obey and abide; ye, even as I." Let us give ourselves to a willing and loving obedience. He will keep us abiding in His love.

Ye, even as I. O my blessed Vine, who makes the branch partaker of Your life and likeness, in this, too, I am to be like You. As Your life in the Father's love is through obedience, so is mine in Your love! Savior, help me, that obedience may indeed be the link between You and me.

Chapter Twenty-Three

JOY

"These things have I spoken unto you, that my joy might remain in you, and that your joy might be full"—John 15:11.

If anyone asks, "How can I be a happy Christian?" our Lord's answer is very simple. He says, "These things," about the Vine and the branches, "I have spoken to you, that my joy might remain in you, and that your joy might be full." In effect, He is saying, "You cannot have My joy without My life. Abide in Me, and let Me abide in you, and My joy will be in you." All healthy life is a thing of joy and beauty. Live the branch life undividedly, and you will have His joy in full measure.

To many Christians, the thought of a life wholly abiding in Christ is one of strain and painful effort. They cannot see that the strain and effort exist only because we do not yield ourselves unreservedly to the life of Christ in us. They have not yet experienced the very first words of the parable: "I am the true Vine. I undertake all and provide for all. I ask nothing of the branch but that it yields wholly to Me, and allows Me to do all. *I engage to make and keep the branch all that it ought to be.*" Should it not be an infinite and unceasing joy to have the Vine thus work all? How glorious to know that it is no one less than the blessed Son of God in His love who is each moment bearing us and maintaining our life!

That My joy might remain in you. We are to have Christ's own joy in us. And what is Christ's own joy? There is no joy like love. There is no joy *but* love. Christ had just spoken of the Father's love, of His own abiding in it, and of His having loved us with that same love. His joy is nothing but the joy of love, of being loved, and of loving. His joy was in receiving His Father's love, abiding in it, passing it on, and then pouring it out on sinners.

He wants to share this joy with us: the joy of being loved of the Father and of Him; the joy of, in our turn, loving and living for those around us. This is the joy of being truly branches—abiding in His love, and then giving up ourselves in love to bear fruit for others. Let us accept His life, as He gives it in us as the Vine. His joy will be ours: the joy of abiding in His love, the joy of loving like Him, of loving with His love.

And that your joy might be full. May it be complete, and may you be filled with it. How sad that we need to be reminded that as God alone is the fountain of all joy, "God our exceeding joy," the only way to be perfectly happy is to have as much of God—as much of His will and fellowship—as possible! Christianity is meant to be a thing of unspeakable joy.

And why do so many complain that it is not so? Because they do not believe that there is no joy like the joy of abiding in Christ and in His love. They do not know the joy of being branches through whom He can pour out His love on a dying world.

Oh, that Christ's voice might reach the heart of every young Christian, and persuade him to believe that His joy is the only true joy. His joy can become ours and truly fill us. And, the sure and simple way of living in it is—only this—to abide as branches in Him our heavenly Vine. Let the truth enter deep into us—as long as our joy is not full, it is a sign that we do not yet know our heavenly Vine completely. Every desire for a fuller joy must only urge us to abide more simply and more fully in His love.

My joy—your joy. In this, too, it is: as the Vine, so the branch; all the Vine in the branch. Your joy is our joy—Your joy in us, and our joy fulfilled. Blessed Lord, fill me with Your joy—the joy of being loved and blessed with a divine love. Give me the joy of loving and blessing others.

Chapter Twenty-Four

LOVE ONE ANOTHER

"This is my commandment, that ye love one another"—John 15:12.

God is love. His whole nature and perfection is love, living not for Himself, but to dispense life and blessing to others. In His love, He begat the Son, that He might give all to Him. In His love, He brought forth man, that He might make them partakers of His blessedness.

Christ is the Son of God's love—the bearer, the revealer, the communicator of that love. His life and death were all love. Love is His life, and the life He gives. He only lives to love, to live out His life of love in us, to give Himself in all who will receive Him. The very first thought of the true Vine is love—living only to impart His life to the branches.

The Holy Spirit is the Spirit of love. He cannot impart Christ's life without imparting His love. Salvation is nothing but love conquering and entering into us. We have just as much of salvation as we have of love. Full salvation is perfect love.

No wonder that Christ said, "A new commandment I give unto you" (John 13:34); "This is my commandment"—the one all-inclusive commandment—"that ye love one another." The branch is not only one with the vine, but with all its other branches. They drink one spirit, form one body, and bear one fruit.

Nothing can be more unnatural than that Christians should not love one another, even as Christ loved them. The life they received from their heavenly Vine is nothing but love. This is the one thing He asks above all others. "By this shall all men know that ye are my disciples. . .love one another" (John 13:35). As the special sort of vine is known by the fruit it bears, the nature of the heavenly Vine is to be judged by the love His disciples have to one another.

See that you obey this commandment. Let your "obey and abide" be seen in this. Love your brethren as the way to abide in the love of your Lord. Let your vow of obedience begin here. Love one another. Let your fellowship with the Christians in your own family be holy, tender, Christlike love. Let your thoughts of the Christians around you be, before everything, in the spirit of Christ's love. Let your life and conduct be the sacrifice of love—give yourself up to think of their sins or their needs. Intercede for them, help and serve them. Be, in your church or circle, the embodiment of Christ's love. The life Christ lives in you is love; let the life in which you live it out be all love.

But, my reader comments, you write as if all this

was so natural and simple and easy. Is it at all possible to thus live and love? My answer is: Christ commands it; you must obey. Christ means it; you must obey, or you cannot abide in His love.

But I have tried and failed. I see no prospect of living like Christ. Ah! that is because you have failed to take in the first word of the parable—"I am the true Vine: I give all you need as a branch. I give all I have myself." I pray, let the sense of past failure and present feebleness drive you to the Vine. He is all love. He loves to give. He gives love. He will teach you to love, even as He loved.

Love one another. Dear Lord Jesus, You are all love. The life You gave us is love. Your new commandment and badge of discipleship is, "Love one another." I accept the charge. With the love with which You love me, and I love You, I will love my brethren.

Chapter Twenty-Five

LOVE AS I HAVE LOVED YOU

"This is my commandment, that ye love one another, as I have loved you"—John 15:12.

This is the second time in this parable that our Lord is our example. The first time it was in His relationship to the Father, keeping His commandments, and abiding in His love. Even so, we are to keep Christ's commandments, and abide in His love. The second time He speaks of His relationship to us as the rule of our love to our brethren. "Love one another, as I have loved you." In each case, His disposition and conduct is to be the law for ours. It is again the truth we have more than once insisted upon—perfect likeness between the Vine and the branch.

Even as I. But is it not a vain thing to imagine that we can keep His commandments, and love the brethren, even as He kept His Father's, and as He loved us? And must not the attempt end in failure and discouragement? Undoubtedly, if we seek to carry it out in our own strength, or without a full understanding of the truth of the Vine and its branches. But if we understand that the "even as I" is the one great lesson of the parable—the one continual language of the Vine to the branch—we will see that it is not a question of what we feel able to accomplish, but of what Christ is able to work in us.

These high and holy commands—"Obey, even as I! Love, as I"—are just meant to bring us to the consciousness of our weakness. Through them, we will be made aware of the need and the beauty and the sufficiency of what is provided for us in the Vine. We will begin to hear the Vine speaking every moment to the branch: "Even as I. Even as I: My life is your life. You have a share in all My fullness. The Spirit in you, and the fruit that comes from you, is all just the same as in Me. Be not afraid, but let your faith grasp each 'Even as I' as the divine assurance that because I live in you, you may and can live like Me."

But why, if this really is the meaning of the parable and the life a branch may live, why do so few realize it? Because they do not know the heavenly mystery of the Vine. They know much about the parable and its beautiful lessons. But, the hidden, spiritual mystery of the Vine in His divine omnipotence and nearness, bearing and supplying them all the day— this they do not know. They have not waited on God's Spirit to reveal it to them.

Love one another, as I have loved you. "Ye, even as I." How are we to begin if we really want to learn the mystery? With the confession that we need to be brought to an entirely new mode of life. We must do so because we have never yet known Christ as the Vine in the completeness of His quickening and transforming power. With the surrender to be cleansed from all that is of self, and detached from all that is in the world, to live only and wholly as Christ lived for the glory of the Father. And then with the faith that this "even as I" is indeed what Christ is ready to make true, the Vine will maintain that very life in the branch wholly dependent on Him.

Even as I. Ever again it is, my blessed Lord, as the Vine, so the branch—one life, one spirit, one obedience, one joy, one love.

Lord Jesus, in the faith that You are my Vine, and that I am Your branch, I accept Your command as a promise, and take Your "even as I" as the simple revelation of what You work in me. Yes, Lord, as You have loved, I will love.

Chapter Twenty-Six

CHRIST'S FRIENDSHIP:
ITS ORIGIN

"Greater love hath no man than this, that a man lay down his life for his friends"—John 15:13.

In this verse and the two following verses, our Lord speaks of His relationship to His disciples in a new aspect—that of friendship. He points us to the love which has its origin on His side (v. 13); to the obedience by which it is maintained on our part (v. 14); and then to the holy intimacy to which it leads (v. 15).

Our relationship to Christ is one of love. In speaking of this previously, He showed us what His love was in its heavenly glory—the same love with which the Father had loved Him. Here we have it in its earthly manifestation—laying down His life for us.

Greater love hath no man than this, that a man lay down his life for his friends. Christ does indeed long to have us know that the secret root and strength of all He is and does for us as the Vine is love. As we learn to believe this, we will feel that here is something which we not only need to think and know about, but a living power—a divine life—which we need to receive within us. Christ and His love are inseparable; they are identical.

God is love, and Christ is love. God and Christ and the divine love can only be known *by having them—by their life and power working within us.* "This is eternal *life*, that they *know* thee." There is no knowing God except by having the life. The life working in us *alone gives the knowledge,* and the love. If we want to know it, we must drink of its living stream. We must have it shed forth in our hearts by the Holy Spirit.

Greater love hath no man than this, that a man lay down his life for his friends. Life is the most precious thing that a man has. His life is all he is; the life is himself. Sacrifice is the highest measure of love. When a man gives his life, he holds nothing back, he gives all he has and is. It is this our Lord Jesus wants to make clear to us concerning His mystery of the Vine. With all He has He has placed Himself at our disposal. He wants us to count Him our very own. He wants to be wholly our possession, so that we may be wholly His possession.

He gave His life for us in death. He did so, not merely as a passing act, that when accomplished was done with, but as a making Himself ours for eternity. Life for life. He gave His life for us to possess that we might give our life for Him to possess. This is what is taught by the parable of the Vine and the branch, in their wonderful identification, in their perfect union.

It is as we know something of this—not by reason

or imagination, but deep down in the heart and life—that we will begin to see what our life as branches of the heavenly Vine ought to be. He gave Himself to death. He lost Himself, that we might find life in Him. This is the true Vine, who only lives to abide in us. This is the beginning and the root of that holy friendship to which Christ invites us.

Great is the mystery of godliness! Let us confess our ignorance and unbelief. Let us cease from our own understanding and our own efforts to master it. Let us wait for the Holy Spirit who dwells within us to reveal it. Let us trust His infinite love, which gave its life for us, to take possession and rejoice in making us wholly its own.

His life for His friends. How wonderful the lessons of the Vine, giving its very life to its branches! And Jesus gave His life for His friends. And that love gives itself to them and in them. My heavenly Vine, oh, teach me how wholly You long to live in me!

Chapter Twenty-Seven

CHRIST'S FRIENDSHIP: ITS EVIDENCE

"Ye are my friends, if ye do whatsoever I command you"—John 15:14.

Our Lord has already said what He gave as proof of His friendship: He gave His life for us. He now tells us what our part is to be—to do the things which He commands. He gave His life to secure a place for His love in our hearts to rule us. The response His love calls us to, and empowers us for, is that we do what He commands us. As we know the dying love, we will joyfully obey its commands. As we obey the commands, we will know the love more fully.

Christ had already said, "If ye keep my commandments, ye shall abide in my love." He thinks this truth is important enough to repeat again. The one proof of our faith in His love, the one way to abide in it, the one mark of being true branches is to do whatsoever He commands us. He began with absolute surrender of His life for us. He can ask nothing less from us. This alone is a life in His friendship.

This truth of the imperative necessity of obedience—doing all that Christ commands us—does not have the place in our Christian teaching and living that Christ meant it to. We have given a far higher place to privilege than to duty. We have not considered implicit obedience a condition of true discipleship. The secret thought that it is impossible to do the things He commands us, and that therefore it cannot be expected of us, combined with a subtle and unconscious feeling that sinning is a necessity, have frequently robbed people of God's promises and their power.

The whole relationship to Christ has become clouded and lowered. The waiting on His teaching, the power to hear and obey His voice, and through obedience to enjoy His love and friendship, have been enfeebled by the terrible mistake. Let us try to return to the true position, take Christ's words as most literally true, and make nothing less the law of our life. "You are My friends, *if you do* the things that I command you." Surely our Lord asks nothing less than that we heartily and truthfully say, "Yes, Lord, what You command, that will I do."

These commands are to be done as a proof of friendship. The power to do them rests entirely in a personal relationship to Jesus. For a friend, I would do what I might not for another. The friendship of Jesus is so heavenly and wonderful. It comes to us as the power of a divine love entering in and taking possession. The unbroken fellowship with Him is so essential to it that it implies and imparts a joy and a love which make the obedience a delight. The liberty to claim the friendship of Jesus, the power to enjoy it, the grace to prove it in all its blessedness all come as we do whatsoever He commands us.

We need to ask our Lord to reveal Himself to us with the dying love in which He proves Himself our friend, and then listen as He says to us, "You are My friends." As we see what our Friend has done for us, and what an unspeakable blessedness it is to have Him call us friends, doing His commands will become the natural fruit of our life in His love. We will not be afraid to say, "Yes, Lord, we are Your friends, and do what You command us."

If ye do. Yes, it is in doing that we are blessed, that we abide in His love, that we enjoy His friendship. "If ye do what I command you!" O my Lord, let Your holy friendship lead me into the love of all Your commands, and let the doing of Your commands lead me ever deeper into Your friendship.

Chapter Twenty-Eight

CHRIST'S FRIENDSHIP: ITS INTIMACY

"Henceforth I call you not servants; for the servant knoweth not what his lord doeth: but I have called you friends; for all things that I have heard of my Father I have made known unto you"—John 15:15.

The highest proof of true friendship, and one great source of its blessedness, is the intimacy which withholds nothing, and allows the friend to share in our innermost secrets. It is a blessed thing to be Christ's servant. His redeemed ones delight to call themselves His slaves. Christ often spoke of the disciples as His servants. In His great love, our Lord now says, "Henceforth I call you not servants." With the coming of the Holy Spirit, a new era was to be inaugurated. "The servant knoweth not what his Lord doeth." He has to obey without being consulted or admitted into the secret of all his master's plans. "*But,* I have called you friends; for all things that I have heard of my Father I have made known unto you." Christ's friends share with Him in all the secrets the Father has entrusted to Him.

Let us think what this means. When Christ spoke of keeping His Father's commandments, He did not mean merely what was written in Holy Scripture. He was also referring to those special commandments which were communicated to Him day by day, and from hour to hour. It was of these He said, "The Father loveth the Son, and sheweth him all things that himself doeth: and he will shew him greater works" (John 5:20). All that Christ did was God's working. God showed it to Christ, so that He could carry out the Father's will and purpose. He did so, not blindly and unintelligently, as man often does, but with full understanding and approval. As one who stood in God's counsel, He knew God's plan.

And this now is the blessedness of being Christ's friends. We do not, as servants, do His will without much spiritual insight into its meaning and aim. But, we are admitted, as an inner circle, into some knowledge of God's more secret thoughts. From the day of Pentecost on, by the Holy Spirit, Christ was to lead His disciples into a spiritual comprehension of the mysteries of the Kingdom. Before this, He had only spoken about them in parables.

Friendship delights in fellowship. Friends hold council. Friends trust each other with things that they would not, for anything, want others to know. What is it that gives a Christian access to this holy intimacy with Jesus? What gives him the spiritual capacity for receiving the communications Christ has to make of what the Father has shown Him? "Ye are My friends *if ye do whatsoever I command you."*

It is loving obedience which purifies the soul. That refers not only to the commandments of the Word, but to that blessed application of the Word to our daily life. No one but our Lord Himself can give that. But as these are waited for in dependence and humility, and faithfully obeyed, the soul becomes fitted for ever-closer fellowship. And, daily friendship may become a continual experience, "I have called you friends...for all things that I have heard of My Father, I have made known unto you."

I have called you friends. What an unspeakable honor! What a heavenly privilege! O Savior, speak the word with power into my soul, "I have called you My friend, whom I love, whom I trust, to whom I make known all that passes between my Father and Me."

Chapter Twenty-Nine

ELECTION

"Ye have not chosen me, but I have chosen you, and ordained you, that ye should go and bring forth fruit"—John 15:16.

The branch does not choose the vine, or decide on which vine it will grow. The vine brings forth the branch, as and where it will. Even so, Christ says, "Ye have not chosen me, but I have chosen you." But some will say that this is the difference between the branch in the natural and in the spiritual world. Man has a will and a power of choosing. It is in virtue of his having decided to accept Christ, his having chosen Him as Lord, that he is now a branch. This is undoubtedly true. And yet it is only a half truth.

The lesson of the Vine, and the teaching of our Lord, point to the other half—the deeper, the divine side of our being in Christ. If He had not chosen us, we would never have chosen Him. Our choosing Him was the result of His choosing us, and taking hold of us. In the very nature of things, it is His prerogative as Vine to choose and create His own branch. We owe all that we are to "the election of grace" (Romans 11:5). Drink deep of this blessed truth, "Ye have not chosen me, but I have chosen you," and you will know Christ as the true Vine, the sole origin and strength of the branch life. You will see yourselves as branches in absolute, most blessed, and most secure dependence on Him.

And why does Christ say this? So that they may know the object for which He chose them, and find, in their faith in His election, the certainty of fulfilling their destiny. Throughout Scripture, this is the great object of the teaching of election. "Predestinate to be conformed to the image of his Son" (to be branches in the image and likeness of the Vine) (Romans 8:29). "Chosen...that we should be holy" (Ephesians 1:4). "Chosen to salvation, through sanctification of the Spirit" (2 Thessalonians 2:13). "Elect...through sanctification of the Spirit unto obedience" (1 Peter 1:2).

Some have abused the doctrine of election. And others, for fear of its abuse, have rejected it because they have overlooked this teaching. They have dwelled on its hidden origin in eternity, with the inscrutable mysteries of the counsels of God, instead of accepting the revelation of its purpose. They do not know about the blessings it brings into our Christian life.

Just think what these blessings are. In our verse, Christ reveals His twofold purpose in choosing us to be His branches. He has done so that we may bear fruit on earth, and have power in prayer in heaven. What confidence the thought that He has chosen us for this gives. He will not fail to prepare us for carrying out His purpose! What assurance that we can bear fruit that will abide, and can pray so as to obtain it! What a continual call to the deepest humility and praise, to the most entire dependence and expectancy! He would not choose us for what we are not fit for, or for what He could not fit us for. He has chosen us; this is the pledge. He will do all in us.

Let us listen in silence of soul to our holy Vine speaking to each of us, "You have not chosen Me!" And let us say, "Yes, Lord, but I choose You now! Amen, Lord!" Ask Him to show you what this means. In Him, the true Vine, your life as branch has its divine origin, its eternal security, and the power to fulfill His purpose. From Him to whose will of love you owe all, you may except all. In Him, His purpose, His power, and His faithfulness, in His love let me abide.

I chose you. Lord, teach me what this means— that You have set Your heart on me, and chosen me to bear fruit that will abide, and to pray prayers that will prevail. In this Your eternal purpose, my soul will find rest and say, "What He chose me for I will be, I can be, I shall be."

Chapter Thirty

ABIDING FRUIT

"I have chosen you, and ordained you, that ye should go and bring forth fruit, and that your fruit should abide"—John 15:16.

There are some fruits that will not keep. Certain kinds of pears or apples must be used at once. Others can be kept until next year. Likewise in Christian work, there is some fruit which does not last. There may be much that pleases and edifies, and yet, no permanent impression is made on the power of the world or the state of the Church.

On the other hand, there is work that leaves its mark for generations or for eternity. In it, the power of God makes itself lastingly felt. This is the fruit which Paul speaks of when he describes the two styles of ministry, "My preaching was not with enticing words of man's wisdom, but in demonstration of the Spirit and of power: that your faith should not stand in the wisdom of men, but in the power of God" (1 Corinthians 2:4-5). The more there is of human wisdom and power, the less there is of stability. The more there is of God's Spirit, the more there is of a faith standing in God's power.

Fruit reveals the nature of the tree from which it comes. What is the secret of bearing fruit that abides? The answer is simple. It is as our life abides in Christ—as we abide in Him—that the fruit we bear will abide. The more we allow human will and effort to be cut down and cleansed away by the divine Husbandman, the more intensely we withdraw from the outward world. Then, God may work in us by His Spirit. That is, the more wholly we abide in Christ, the more will our fruit abide.

What a blessed thought! He chose you, and ordained you to bear fruit, *and your fruit should abide.* He never meant for one of His branches to bring forth fruit that should not abide. The deeper I enter into the purpose of this His electing grace, the surer my confidence that I can bring forth fruit to eternal life—for myself and others. The deeper I enter into the purpose of His electing love, the more I will realize that abiding in Him is the link between the purpose *from* eternity, and the fruit *to* eternity. The purpose is His; He will carry it out. The fruit is His; He will bring it forth. The abiding is His; He will maintain it.

Let everyone who professes to be a Christian worker, pause. Ask whether you are leaving your mark for eternity on those around you. It is not your preaching or teaching, your strength of will or power to influence, that will secure this. *All depends on having your life full of God and His power.* And that depends on your truly living the branch-like life of abiding—very close and unbroken fellowship with Christ. It is the branch which abides in Him that brings forth much fruit—fruit that will abide.

Blessed Lord, reveal to my soul that You have chosen me to bear much fruit. Let this be my confidence—that Your purpose can be realized— You did choose me. Let this be my power to forsake everything and give myself to You. You will perfect what You have begun. Draw me to so dwell in the love and the certainty of that eternal purpose that the power of eternity may possess me, and the fruit I bear may abide.

That ye may bear fruit. O my heavenly Vine, it is beginning to dawn upon my soul that fruit, more fruit—much fruit—abiding fruit is the one thing You have to give me, and the one thing as a branch I have to give You. Here I am. Blessed Lord, work out Your purpose in me. Let me bear much fruit, abiding fruit, to Your glory.

Chapter Thirty-One

PREVAILING PRAYER

"I ordained you, that ye should go and bring forth fruit, and that your fruit should abide: that what-soever ye shall ask of the Father in my name, he may give it you"—John 15:16.

In the first verse of our parable, Christ revealed Himself as the true Vine, and the Father as the Husbandman. He asked that we keep a place in our heart for Himself and the Father. Here, in the closing verse, He sums up all His teaching concerning Himself and the Father in stating the twofold purpose for which He had chosen them.

With reference to Himself, the Vine, the purpose was that they should bear fruit. With reference to the Father, it was that whatsoever they should ask in His name, should be done by the Father in heaven. As fruit is the greatest proof of a true relationship to Christ, so prayer is proof of our relationship to the Father. A fruitful abiding in the Son and prevailing prayer to the Father are the two greatest factors in the true Christian life.

That whatsoever ye shall ask of the Father in My name, He may give it you. These are the closing words of the parable of the Vine. The whole mystery of the Vine and its branches leads up to this other mystery—that *whatsoever we ask in His name the Father gives!* Here is the reason for the lack of prayer, and the lack of power in prayer. It is because we rarely live the true branch life that we do not feel constrained to much prayer. It is because we so seldom lose ourselves in the Vine that we do not feel confident that we will be heard. And, because it is so unusual for us to abide in Him entirely, we do not know how to use His name as the key to God's storehouse.

The Vine planted on earth has reached up into heaven. It is only the soul wholly and intensely abiding in it that can reach into heaven with power to prevail much. Our faith in the teaching and the truth of the parable—in the truth and the life of the Vine—must prove itself by power in prayer. The life of abiding and obedience, of love and joy, of cleansing and fruitbearing, will surely lead to the power of prevailing prayer.

Whatsoever ye shall ask. The promise was given to the disciples when they were ready to give themselves, in the likeness of the true Vine, for their fellow men. This promise was their provision for their work. They took it literally; they believed it; they used it; and they found it to be true. Let us give ourselves, as branches of the true Vine, and in His likeness, to the work of saving men. Let us bring forth fruit to the glory of God, and we will find a new urgency and power to pray and to claim the "whatsoever ye ask." We will awaken to our wonderful responsibility of having been promised the keys to the King's storehouses. And, we will not rest until we have received bread and blessing for the perishing.

¹ "I have chosen you...that ye should go and bring forth fruit, and that your fruit should abide: that whatsoever ye shall ask of the Father in My name, He may give it you." Beloved disciple, seek, above everything, to be a man of prayer. Here is the highest exercise of your privilege as a branch of the Vine. Here is the full proof of your being renewed in the image of God and His Son. Here is your power to show how you, like Christ, live not for yourself, but for others. Here you enter into heaven to receive gifts for men. Here your abiding in Christ has led to His abiding in you—to use you as the channel and instrument of His grace. The power to bear fruit for men has been crowned by power to prevail with God.

"I am the true Vine, and my Father is the Husbandman." Christ's work in you is to bring you to the Father, so that His word may be fulfilled in you, "At that day ye shall ask in my name: and I say not unto you, that I will pray the Father for you: for the Father himself loveth you" (John 16:26-27). The power of direct access to the Father for men, the liberty of intercession claiming and receiving blessing for them in faith, is the highest exercise of our union with Christ. Let all who truly and fully want to be branches give themselves to the work of intercession. It is the one great work of Christ the Vine in heaven—the source of power for all His work. Make it your one great work as a branch. It will be the power of all your work.

In My name. Yes, Lord, in your name, the new name You have given Yourself here, the true Vine. As a branch, abiding in You in entire devotion, in full dependence, in perfect conformity, and in abiding fruitfulness, I come to the Father, in You, and He will give what I ask. Oh, let my life be one of unceasing and prevailing abiding in the Vine.

ABOUT THE AUTHOR

Andrew Murray (1828-1917) was an amazingly prolific Christian author. He lived and ministered as both a pastor and a writer from the towns and villages of South Africa. All of his publications were originally written in Dutch and then translated into English. As his popularity grew, Murray's books found their way into more than twelve foreign languages during his lifetime alone.

Andrew Murray's early writings were primarily written for the edification of the believer—building them up in faith, love and prayer. They include *Abide in Christ, The Spirit of Christ,* and *With Christ in the School of Prayer.* Later writings leaned more heavily upon the sanctification of the believer with such works as *Holy in Christ* and *Be Perfect.* Finally, in his last days, Murray addressed the issue of the Church and its lack of power in the earth. He emphasized the need for a constant and vital relationship with Jesus Christ and for consistent, fervent prayer.

Murray was an alert and intense man, continuing on in his writings until his death at age eighty-nine. His burning desire to transpose all that lay on his heart and spirit to paper was revealed in the presence of several manuscripts in various stages of completion at the time of his death.

Andrew Murray has greatly blessed the Christian world with the richness of his spiritual wisdom and his ability to see and answer the needs of God's people.